ANNA-STINA LINDÉN IVARSSON
KATARINA BRIEDITIS
KATARINA EVANS

TRANSLATED BY MARIA LUNDIN

# SECOND-TIME COOL

## THE ART OF CHOPPING UP A SWEATER

ANNICK PRESS

TORONTO + NEW YORK + VANCOUVER

© 2005 Annick Press Ltd.

First published in Sweden by Alfabeta Bokförlag as *Do Redo* © 2004 Anna-Stina Lindén, Katarina Brieditis, and Katarina Evans

The authors wish to thank the models who volunteered their time for the book as well as the individuals who supplied accessories.

We acknowledge the support of the Canada Council for the Arts, the Ontario Arts Council, and the Government of Canada through the Book Publishing Industry Development Program (BPIDP) for our publishing activities.

Translated by Maria Lundin
Copy edited by Elizabeth McLean
Project management by Antonia Banyard
Cover and interior design by Irvin Cheung/iCheung Design
Cover photograph by Waldemar Hansson

Special thanks to Guy, who took all photos of the craft items in the book, and to Venessa Bentley of Working Hands Knitwear Design and Instruction for craft and textile expertise for this edition.

**Published in the U.S.A. by**
Annick Press (U.S.) Ltd.

**Distributed in Canada by**
Firefly Books Ltd.
66 Leek Crescent
Richmond Hill, ON
L4B 1H1

**Distributed in the U.S.A. by**
Firefly Books (U.S.) Inc.
P.O. Box 1338
Ellicott Station
Buffalo, NY 14205

**Cataloguing in Publication**
Lindén Ivarsson, Anna-Stina
        Second-time cool : the art of chopping up a sweater / by Anna-Stina Lindén Ivarsson, Katarina Brieditis and Katarina Evans ; translated by Maria Lundin. — North American ed.

Translation of: Do redo : konsten att slakta en tröja.
ISBN 1-55037-911-9 (bound).—ISBN 1-55037-910-0 (pbk.)

        1. Clothing and dress—Remaking—Juvenile literature.
2. Knitting—Juvenile literature. 3. Crocheting—Juvenile literature.
I. Brieditis, Katarina II. Evans, Katarina III. Title.

TT820.L55 2005          646.4'08          C2005-902569-7

The text was typeset in Meta and Bokka

Printed and bound in China

Visit our website at **www.annickpress.com**

# CONTENTS

# Foreword

Clothes announce your personality, your identity. Clothes allow us to play, change styles, and become someone different. With *Second-Time Cool,* you'll see how easy it is to make things with your own hands: how you can make new from old with craft techniques people have used through the ages, and how you can be sure no one else has clothing exactly like yours.

Just take an old wool sweater, put it in the wash on the hot cycle, and make something new. Don't be inhibited by rules and convention—let your hands lead the way and inspiration will follow. Get those scissors chopping! That old sweater will be transformed, even if the result is not what you imagined at the beginning. Ideas are everywhere: on TV, on the street, in the stores, in old books and magazines ... even in museums. The way people used to do things is a great way to ignite your imagination.

Working with your hands is fun. And it's good for your soul. New ideas are often born when your hands are busy. You don't have to work fast. Be sure to enjoy the process, and forget about any pressure to perform —there are no rules. You're in charge!

Sweater, headscarf, mitts, and bag—all
made from recycled sweaters and decorated
with embroidery. The sweater was cut open
and shortened in front and the arms length-
ened using the extra material. The bag's
lining is an unfinished cross-stitch project
found in a second-hand store. The bag's
fringe is made with reflective elastic.

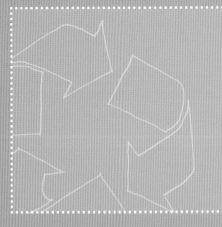

# REUSE & RECYCLE

There are lots of good reasons to buy clothes second-hand. To begin, it's a cheap way to find something unusual and unique.

Second, it's good for the environment. Why buy new stuff when so many quality used items are available?

Third, remember that when you shop in second-hand outlets operated by charitable organizations, your shopping dollars help people in need.

Last but not least, you and your friends can have a lot of fun rummaging through racks and bargain bins to rediscover earlier fashions. Today, everything is retro, whether we're recycling trends from the '50s, '60s, '70s, or '80s. Still, there are always details you can change to create your own distinctive style. Fashion builds on its past, and time, together with your personal touch, adds unique twists.

This is a chance for your creativity to shine. You can mend, alter, and cut up second-hand clothes without fear. Don't worry, you can afford to make mistakes when you're chopping up a sweater.

## Recycling used to be natural

In past generations, people saved and reused worn-out things. Resources and raw materials were scarce and often expensive. Thrift was a virtue, and producing new clothes took significant effort. The sheep had to be sheared, the material woven, and the garment sewn. Buying something ready-made was impossible for most people: retail stores were rare.

A tattered sweater would never be thrown out; it would have been mended again and again. When it couldn't be repaired anymore, the wool would be chopped into small pieces, the yarn bits ground up, then mixed with new wool, and finally spun into new yarn. When the patches on clothes couldn't hold the garment together any longer, larger pieces were kept and made into children's clothes. Smaller rags were used for patchwork, as decorative elements on bags, for padding cushions, or for stuffing into cracks to insulate the house. Linen clothes could even be made into paper.

Colorful rugs displayed on festive occasions used to be popular in the homes of rich European farmers. Around the mid-1800s, less wealthy people imitated the practice, which ushered in the rag rug trend. Rag rugs were woven out of old clothes and material that had been cut into thin strips. Quilts were also a popular way to decorate the home—and to use up odd bits of cloth.

With so much recycling going on, we find very few antique garments preserved today.

## countless tons of clothes in our landfills

Not many people take the time to patch, mend, or even make rags out of worn-out clothes anymore. Today we throw them out or donate them to charity and buy new ones.

Every year, charities across North America collect tons and tons of clothes. Some of them are sold in thrift shops here at home, while some are given to aid organizations to distribute in needy areas around the globe.

Most of the clothing comes from well-known stores and brands—but many shops also end up with some unusual brands and wonderful old originals. With a little imagination, thrift shoppers can make amazing finds!

## Vintage: a timely fashion

In the last few years, vintage boutiques have appeared in major cities, selling handpicked items from specific time periods or style eras.

A growing number of fashion designers are also remaking old garments—known as "customization." This process can be as radical as a total change of cut and form, or as simple as a change of hemline.

One of the first fashion creators to work in this spirit was Vivienne Westwood, born in 1941. Together with her husband, Malcolm McLaren, she created punk as a life and clothing style. Their boutique in London, England, which still exists today, quickly became famous. There, Vivienne sold creative T-shirts

A jewelry maker combines old textiles with silver, turning embroidered tablecloths into chokers and bracelets.

Shoes used to be altered according to the newest fashions. These boots from the 1800s were spiffed up with new decorative cloth flowers and higher heels.

throughout the '70s. She colored, sliced, and ripped up the shirts. She printed provocative slogans on them and gave them all kinds of stitched-on detailing. People who couldn't afford to buy her shirts went home and made their own.

Martin Margiela, born in Belgium in 1959, was among the first to show second-hand clothes on the catwalk in Paris. The designer is a sort of haute couture hobo, infamous for his originality and unconventional attitude to the world of fashion.

Now, Margiela has become a cult avant-garde figure for the sustainability trend.

His designs embrace a broader ideal of beauty than we usually see in high fashion. "One size fits all" is a notion he has explored often, and reused materials almost always form part of his collections. Recently, Margiela showed jackets and pants in recycled leather, worn over traditional Norwegian cardigans turned inside out.

Office supply boa. Fashion design students often use unlikely materials in unexpected ways. Here, thousands of elastics have been tied to a strip of weave instead of yarn or feathers. They're packed so tightly, this boa is heavy to wear.

Extreme reuse. Every inch of these pants from the 1800s is darned or patched.

Traditional quilting technique inspired John Galliano's giant crinoline. Note the recycled Coke cans in the hairstyle!

An innovative line of designer clothing, TRAID Remade, creates one-off garments out of second-hand clothes. These jersey knit tops are updated with appliqué. The teardrop skirt mixes and matches vintage fabrics.

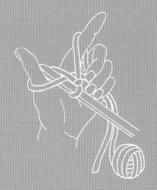

# WOOL IS UNBEATABLE

In this book, we'll work with wool, one of the world's most ancient natural materials.

**W**ool fiber has many extraordinary properties. As appealing as Gore-Tex, fleece, and other high-tech innovations may be, few materials can beat wool. Its properties cannot be reproduced artificially.

For a start, wool is very effective at retaining body heat. It can absorb a lot of moisture before it feels cold to the touch, a quality that has saved many people from freezing to death. Only wool can keep you warm even when it's completely soaked.

Its ability to absorb moisture also prevents static electricity from building up, so wool doesn't attract lint and dust from the air, and stays clean longer.

Although wool absorbs moisture, liquids roll right off the surface, thanks to tiny scales on the outside of the fiber. Good news for the accident prone …

Wool has more natural elasticity than any other fiber, so it's more comfortable to wear and keeps its original appearance longer than most other fabrics. Each wool fiber is made of millions of "coiled springs" that stretch instead of breaking. You can fold, crumple, and compress wool, and it springs right back.

And wool is naturally safe and non-flammable, so it doesn't need to be chemically treated.

## Felting and rolling
When combined with heat and moisture, wool felts together. Felting is an ancient technique that is still used all over the world. Felt-makers often start with unspun wool and knead it in soapy water. After a few steps, the fabric is rolled, and the end result is a dense, compact wool blanket.

Felt is resistant to both wind and moisture. It is a true survival material that can be made into a wide range of items: covers, carpets, and bedspreads, as well as shoes, hats, and mitts.

In 1946, when the bikini was invented in France, it was a symbol of the liberation felt after Nazi Occupation. In America, a more modest version was worn, with a halter top and shorts, so that the navel remained covered.

The original bikinis were knit, like the 1949 models pictured above, and are still popular. Today, however, new elastic yarns mean that they will stay on if you decide to take a swim.

Japanese designer Jun Takahashi for Undercover weathers wool in his workshop to create the used feel in this unique ensemble.

A dress constructed from several felted, chopped sweaters in a series of blue tones. The necklace has been updated with flowers crocheted in mohair.

# THE ART OF CHOPPING UP A SWEATER

An old sweater becomes a vest with plaid wool appliqué.

**Now the fun begins. Before you start, you must wash your sweater in hot water so the wool will felt up. Then the material will turn into a tight weave that you can cut up without it unraveling.**

Your sweater should preferably be 100% wool so it will felt up to the desired degree, and go from being a stretchy knit to an inelastic fabric.

Thin wool sweaters, such as lamb's wool pullovers, turn into smooth, supple felt, good for skirts or wrist warmers. Thick wool sweaters become stiffer and tougher when washed, better for making sturdy items like a pair of slippers or a bag.

## The chopping block— sharpen your scissors!

Lay your sweater on a table and find the sharpest scissors you have. Look at your raw material and let the ideas start to flow. You have lots of options, from a single-step change like cutting off sleeves to make a vest, to a multi-step total remake. You might even turn two sweaters into one by lengthening the sleeves, splicing the bottom, and adding decorative touches.

For making smaller accessories, keep in mind that you can incorporate existing seams into the design. For example, you can turn a neckline into a "necklace." A sleeve can be altered to make a wrist warmer, a leg warmer, or a mitten. The midriff can become a skirt, and the turtleneck a hat.

Challenge yourself to see how

many things you can create out of one sweater!

Of course, you can also chop up your sweater completely and use the pieces like you would any material. That's how to make the slippers, mitts, and bags in the following chapters.

In general, you won't need to leave as much seam allowance as you might be used to, because felt stretches and takes the shape of whatever is inside it (like your hand).

As with any project, it's always best to pin the design together first and try it on before you sew it.

# Washing a wool sweater

If a sweater has lost its elasticity, you might want to just change its detailing. This sweater was cut open in front and up the sleeves, and trimmed using colorful zippers.

A seafarer sweater turned inside out becomes a tote bag.

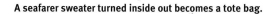

Black leg warmers have elastic bands at the top, decorated with fringe trim. The white stripes on the skirt are unraveled sweater yarn, attached with couching stitch.

White sweater sleeves have been transformed into leg warmers, dressed up with embroidery and tassels. A white fisherman's sweater turns into a skirt, decorated with half-moon crochet edging.

The red leg warmers were spliced at the top, and buttons and ruffled edging added. The red skirt, too, was edged with a ruffle in a thinner material and adorned with chain stitch and fake pearls.

Keep legs and backsides warm!

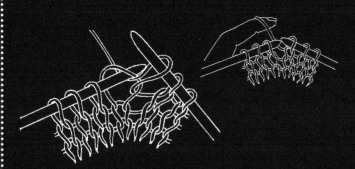

# PROJECT IDEAS

Skirt made from a lamb's wool sweater turned upside-down. The trim is taken from a patterned sweater, and sewn on with blanket stitch.

### Wrist Warmers

Wrist warmers are the simplest way to start—they don't even need to be sewn together. Take advantage of the cuff the sweater already has. Pull on the sleeve the "wrong" way, then measure however long you think the wrist warmer should be and cut it off. Next, decorate it with embroidery, a fringe, beads—or whatever you think up.

### Leg Warmers

If your sweater sleeves didn't shrink as much, you can make leg warmers out of them. Cut the sleeves off at the length you prefer – if they're too short, you can add material at the top. If they're too tight around the calves, add one or two "wedges" by slitting the sleeves open and sewing on strips of another material. After that, decorate with anything you like!

### Skirts

Making a skirt is easy. Turn a sweater upside down, with the bottom cuff hugging your waist. Cut off at the armpits and, just like that, you have a miniskirt. If you want a longer skirt, trim with another material, or sew or knit ruffles onto it, then embellish to your heart's content.

Kaya shows off the skirt she made at a workshop she organized with her friends.

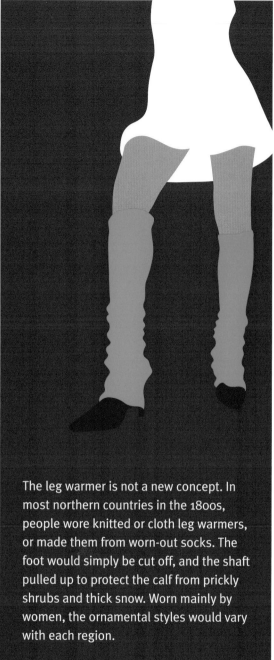

The leg warmer is not a new concept. In most northern countries in the 1800s, people wore knitted or cloth leg warmers, or made them from worn-out socks. The foot would simply be cut off, and the shaft pulled up to protect the calf from prickly shrubs and thick snow. Worn mainly by women, the ornamental styles would vary with each region.

Wrist warmer decorated with fringe trim and bead embroidery.

Wrist warmer with wool appliqué flowers.

Wrist warmers with cut fringe and bead embroidery.

Wrist warmer with sewn-on flaps made of colorful felt.

Vest and hat, like all of the mittens on the clothesline, are made from chopped-up wool sweaters.

## Mittens

Here are two ways of sewing mittens. Pick which to use based on the width of your sweater sleeve.

### Mitten with a whole thumb

Slip on the sleeve the "wrong" way, and position the cuff around your wrist.

Now you need to see if there is enough room to make a whole thumb. If you can move your fingers around easily, you can sew the mitt and the thumb in one piece. Separate your thumb from your other fingers inside the sleeve and make sure there's enough seam allowance between thumb and fingers to both cut and sew.

Pin around your own hand, then cut out the mitten shape, following the pins. Place this shape in reverse on the other sleeve, lining up the cuffs, and cut to create another identical shape, but with the thumb on the opposite side.

Sew up both mittens, following the instructions on the next page.

### Mitten with thumb attached

If you don't have enough room to make a thumb in the sweater sleeve, you can make a mitten with an attached thumb.

Stick your hand in the sleeve. Mark where the thumb should be attached, then cut a suitably sized opening. Push your thumb through the hole, then cut out the mitten shape, ready for sewing.

Mittens with thumb in one piece. Here, the sweater cuff has been reused on the mitt.

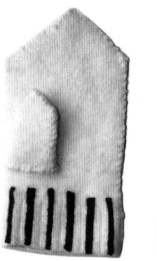

Mittens with attached thumb and classic red appliqué.

Make a pattern for these used-sweater gloves by splitting open an old leather glove. These LOVE-HATE gloves and the polka-dot glove are embroidered with satin stitch.

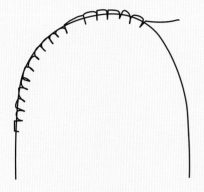

**Blanket stitch**

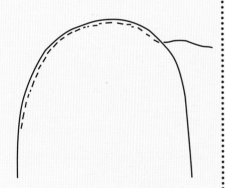

**Running stitch**

Next, measure the width of the thumb slit and the length of your thumb. Cut out a thumb from another part of the sweater—it's more stylish if you round the top to match the shape of your thumb.

First, sew the thumb together, and then attach it to the mitt, following the instructions on the next page.

### Stitching up your mitten

You can choose between several types of stitches, depending on the look you want for your mittens (refer to pages 50 to 54).

The easiest way is to sew small, simple top stitches or running stitches with regular thread in a color that matches the mitten. They'll blend in with the material and be nearly invisible. Then you can turn the mitten the other way out and decide how to decorate.

If you want a visible seam, you can sew the mitten together with blanket stitch and leave it facing out. With this method, you can choose a coarser thread in an accent color so the seam becomes an decorative element, too.

An accident resulted in the first felted wool mittens. In the mid-1800s, a woman living north of the Arctic Circle knit a pair of mitts using a coarse, raw wool yarn. Unsatisfied with the result, she tried to make them better by rubbing and rolling them in soapy water, after which they became fuzzy, soft and extremely warm. First considered bulky and awkward, the mittens gained popularity because of their warmth. These mittens—named Lovikka-mittens after the village in which the woman lived and where they are still produced— remain popular today.

24

All of these hats have been crafted from recycled sweaters.

1970s World Cup skiing champion Ingemar Stenmark sported his own toque style. Even Hollywood stars have caught on to knitting, from Julia Roberts to Sarah Jessica Parker to Russell Crowe. The hat worn by Julia Roberts in the movie *Stepmom* has been copied by thousands of knitting fans.

## Hats

Today, knitted hats, called toques, and caps have replaced fedoras and bonnets as creative expressions of head-warming style. Think of a pop star whose image includes a signature toque or cap …

The toque has a special history. In France, a red toque became a symbol of the 1789 revolution. During World War II, European soldiers could be identified by the color of their toque. In Canada, the early Voyageurs included toques among their essential gear, as they traveled the continent by canoe in search of furs.

Locally patterned hats have been knit by hand for a long time in northern Europe and Scandinavia. During the 1970s, world-famous ski racer Ingemar Stenmark popularized a uniquely patterned wool hat, created by his mother, which caught on all over the Western world.

The simplest hat is sewn together from two pieces of material. Measure the circumference of your head and divide by two. Also measure how high your head is from the bottom of your ears (that's probably where you want the hat to sit). It's a good idea to draw the pattern on paper using your measurements. You can make the top round or pointed.

Place the pattern in the bottom corner of a washed sweater. If the sweater has a good cuff, it can be used as an extra detail – plus it will hug your head nicely. If not, place your pattern just above the cuff and add seam allowance. If you want to leave the seam face out, you won't need as big an allowance. It's better to cut too large than too small, though—you can always alter it if the hat ends up too big.

Cut out the pattern through both sides of the sweater so you get two halves. Pin them together and try the hat on before you sew it up, using a running stitch or backstitch.

Now you can dress the hat up any way that suits your style.

A super-simple variant on the hat is a headscarf: just cut a triangle and decorate.

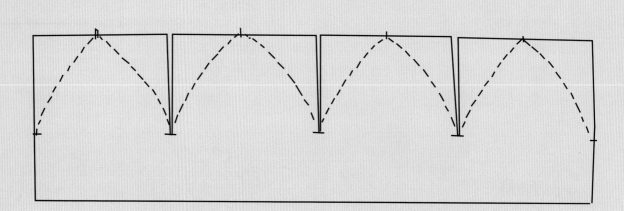

**If you want a round top on your hat, enlarge this pattern to create an iron shape.**

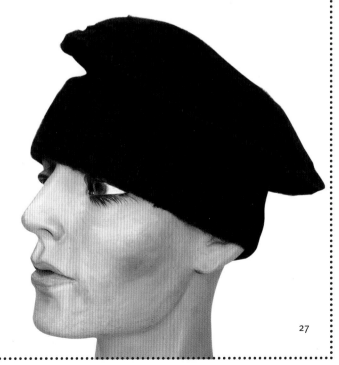

A sweater waistband is cut the right size to fit snugly around the crown of the head. The cap part contains a half-moon piece of heavy cardboard, its shape copied from an old baseball cap. The cardboard is slipped between two sewn-together pieces of cloth, and sewn onto the hat front using running stitch or blanket stitch. The skull-and-bones is a combination of embroidery and appliqué.

Hat with cuff made from two parts of a sweater, sewn together using blanket stitch.

Black hat made using an upside-down turtleneck with a "lid" attached.

27

Hat made using the iron-shaped pattern on page 26, with chain-stitch embroidery, backstitch, and stem stitch.

Iron-shaped "faux-fur" hat with earflaps. Fluffy yarn ends tied on give a furry effect.

Toque made from a turtleneck, and embroidered with reflective material and beads.

Headscarf with a rounded seam, with sewn-on chinstraps and classic cross-stitch embroidery.

Headscarf made from two leftover sweater pieces, featuring strips of white cloth attached with running stitch.

Headscarf with metal buttons and thick silver thread embroidery.

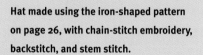

Spiff up an ordinary brown wool headband with a cloth flower, from designers Dolce and Gabbana.

Ancient Inca design probably inspired this bold hat in primary colors from designer John Galliano for Dior.

Homemade ballerina outfits. Slippers, purses, and tops are all made from chopped-up sweaters.

Express your personal style from your head to the tip of your toes. Slippers not only complete an outfit, but will keep your feet warm in the winter. You can even make extra pairs for visitors!

**Sports fan slippers. The appliqué is underlain with reflective material: easy to find in the dark!**

**Sneaker-themed slippers, adorned with toe-shields, stripes from a white ribbed sweater, and string to adjust the fit.**

## Slippers

Here are patterns for two different kinds of slippers: one ballet style and one simple slide slipper.

### Slide slippers

Choose the thickest sweater you have. Draw an outline of your largest foot (everybody has one foot slightly bigger than the other) on a piece of paper, then cut out the pattern. Follow the pattern (you won't need seam allowance for the soles) on the thick sweater to cut out one sole, then flip the pattern over and cut out the other foot's sole. For extra thick slippers, make two of each sole that you can sew together.

Next, measure the top of your foot. Start from the inside of the ankle to the outside; then, starting at the front of the toes, measure toward the ankle as far as you want the slipper to reach. Mark these two measurements on a piece of sweater (you won't need a pattern for the tops), cut a rectangle, then drape the rectangle over the top of your foot. You might need to adjust the fit at this point, and remember to leave a seam allowance for the top. Now flip the top over on another piece of sweater, and copy the cut to make the second foot top.

Before you sew, pin the pieces together, starting from the front and continuing back on both sides. Try it on and make adjustments if you need to. Sew up the slippers—a simple running stitch works well.

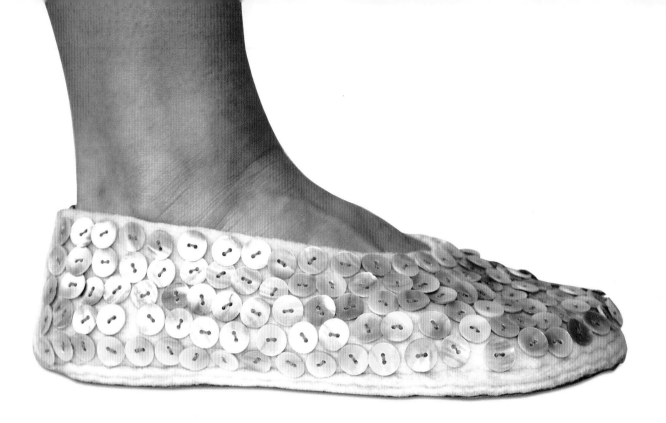

## Ballet slippers

For these slippers, a sweater that is neither too thin nor too thick works best.

Use the pattern on the opposite page; enlarge with a photocopier as needed, and reverse it to create the left foot. You won't need to add seam allowance—it's included in the pattern. Double the bottom pieces to make two-layered soles; thick soles are more comfortable. The most suitable part of the sweater for the soles is the sleeves. Use the body of the sweater for slipper tops.

Fold the edge of the top piece inward and pin the resulting inside lip to the outer edge of the sole, starting at the front and moving toward the back. The top pattern should allow for some overlap at the heel, which will add stability to the slipper.

Sew the pieces together with a running or basting stitch.

Next, turn the slipper inside out and sew down the edge of the seam allowance to the sole. This will make your slipper more comfy. Then you're ready to decorate your slipper with tassels, beads, pom-poms, or mother-of-pearl buttons (as shown above).

••••••••••••••••••••••••••••••••••••••••••

Silk ballerina slippers with pointed toes from 1800, decorated with a reverse style of appliqué.

Today, the ballet slipper is the height of fashion, just as it was in the 1950s. That wasn't the first time, either: 200 years ago, fashion called for flat, dainty shoes with rosettes or long straps to tie up over the ankle—all inspired by ancient style.

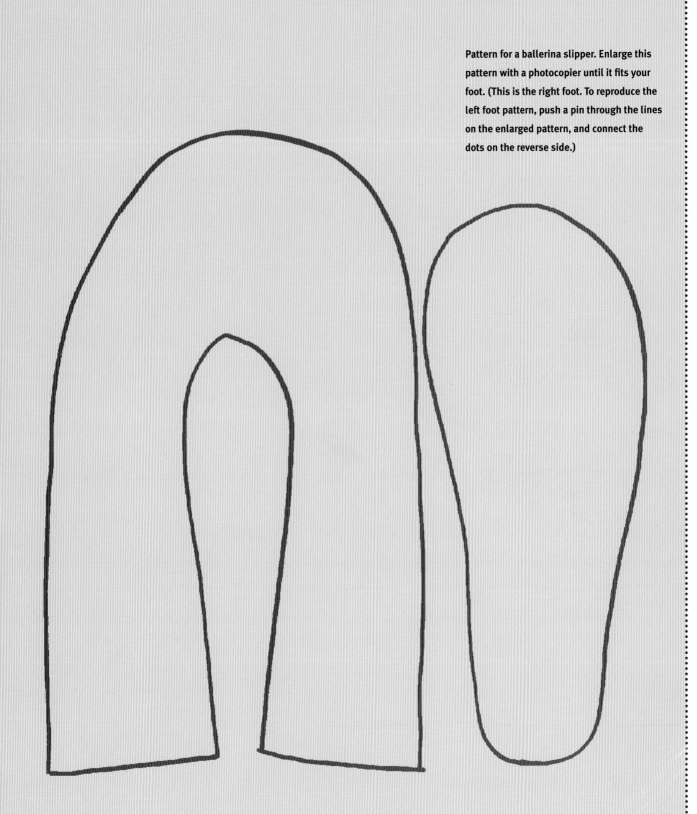

Pattern for a ballerina slipper. Enlarge this pattern with a photocopier until it fits your foot. (This is the right foot. To reproduce the left foot pattern, push a pin through the lines on the enlarged pattern, and connect the dots on the reverse side.)

Bag and gloves made from recycled sweaters. "Fur" hat created with the knitting pattern on pages 68–69.

This shot pouch is made from dark wool cloth and decorated with floral beadwork and ribbon — an example of the craftsmanship of the Naskapi, an Innu nation in Québec.

## Bags

Handbags are always an important fashion accessory. Every serious fashion house presents new purse models in spring and fall.

Bag making is an area where your imagination really is the only limit. You just need to make sure there's room somewhere to put stuff – large or small. Check out antique purses, which are like small drawstring sacks. They're feminine in style, often artfully decorated with needlework and appliqué using colored wool.

Small bags made from a variety of textiles. The three on the left are old, and the one on the right is new, inspired by the sack-purse style.

**1.**

**2.**

**3.**

**4.**

1. Bag where the waistband forms a decorative element at the top. Floral embroidery in chain stitch, stem stitch, and backstitch.

2. Chanel-styled bag made from a thick sweater in fancy, melee yarn. The seams are reinforced with elastic bands, and the closure features decorative chain and yarn pompoms.

3. Simple tote bag from two large squares, with a thick braid for a handle.

4. Purse with small cloth roses in appliqué.

5. Shoulder bag made from a patterned sweater, with fringe trim.

6. Shoulder bag made using traditional Scottish knit sweater, with silver beads sewn on at edge.

7. Spotted tote with a silk pull-cord. Large dots appliquéd using blanket stitch.

**5.**

**6.**

**7.**

Before and after: The cut of the sweater determined the shape of this shopping bag. Made from a thick, felted sweater.

Two sweaters become one. Hers was created by cutting off a beige wool turtleneck around the neck and at the bottom, then embellishing the new neckline, and lengthening the sleeves with a brown sweater. His hat and tie are also created from reused wool.

## Sweaters

Even an old, unfashionable sweater can be altered or remade in any number of ways. Since it will shrink when you wash it, you may need an additional sweater or more for splicing and lengthening. Differences in color or material don't matter—use contrasts to create fun accents. The following pages show some ideas to get you started.

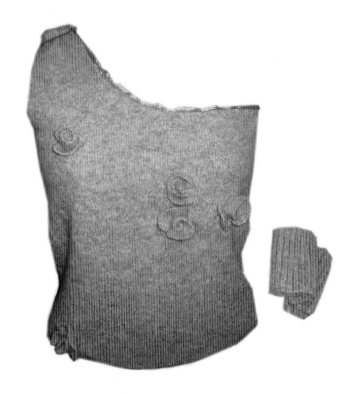

A worn, shrunken, moth-eaten sweater is transformed into a tank top. A sliding buckle on the right shoulder adjusts the fit. The neckline is reinforced with a thin lace ribbon, and cloth roses hide the moth holes. The cuffs were kept so they could be worn as accessories with the tank.

This sweater didn't felt up as desired. So instead, the cuffs were cut off and replaced with a crocheted border. Attaching thin elastic band on the inside (with a zigzag stitch to form a casing) created the elastic effect. The dots are sewn-on crocheted circles.

The sleeves were cut off and the neckline widened on this sweater, transforming it into a T-shirt, which was then decorated with appliqué in dark blue felt and stem stitch embroidery.

Tank top made from a V-neck lamb's wool vest. The neck strap was strengthened using the stretchy trim from around the armholes. "Sequined" peace sign created with mother-of-pearl buttons.

Dress assembled by joining together strips of several different sweaters using running stitch.

# Neck warmers

The traditional scarf has been joined by new ways to keep your neck warm. A neck warmer can be any shape. The simplest type can be made by cutting off the neck on a turtleneck.

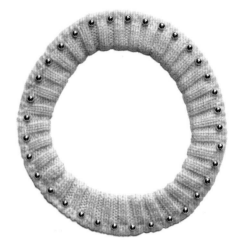

**A combination neck warmer and necklace, decorated with silver beads.**

**Three sweaters braided together and fastened with a few stitches.**

**Neck collar with colorful wooly buttons.**

Two felted sweaters sewn together into a scarf, with a series of rows of running stitch in silver thread.

Chopped-off turtleneck, with bottom and top cut to make two fringes.

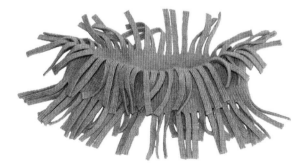

Tie made from the V-neck and front of a lamb's wool sweater.

The small details make the ensemble, such as the flower embroidery on the lower part of these sleeves. From John Galliano, a British fashion designer working in Paris.

# EMBROIDERY

**Humorous design on this evening gown, with rose appliqué and embroidery after a drawing by Jean Cocteau. Drawing by Elsa Shiaparelli, 1937.**

For centuries, embroidery was considered one of the best skills for young women to learn. A home with beautiful textiles was a rich home, and a woman with superior needlework was highly admired.

## Making art into embroidery

Elsa Shiaparelli (1890–1973) was an Italian fashion pioneer with a great sense of humor and ingenuity. Her designs were meant to amuse and provoke, and they often succeeded. She is famous, among other things, for her shoe-shaped hat, as well as her gold-studded gloves and music-box purse.

Elsa worked with some of the leading artists of her day. She interpreted their drawings in splendid clothing embroidery designs, made in Paris by the famed embroidery studio, Lesage. Since the end of the 1800s through to today, the Lesage family has embroidered for the great haute couture houses, where every garment is sewn by hand and often enhanced with beads, pearls, or gems.

All over the world people have historically embellished their clothes with embroidery. Fashion designers are continually inspired by this immense variety of national traditions.

## Sending a message with embroidery

Like many other art forms, embroidered images can contain hidden meanings or serve as coded messages. In the late 1500s, for example, Mary Queen of Scots was held prisoner at Tutbury Castle in England. During her fifteen years there, she passed the time on many needlework projects. Sometimes, the images she embroidered were meant as veiled insults to enemies, or as allusions to Queen Elizabeth I, her cousin and captor. By sending these beautiful gifts to Elizabeth or others, Mary was also expressing her frustration at being held prisoner. Whether decorative or political, your own embroidery can be beautiful and expressive.

## Why wear other brands—when you have your own?

Today, we collect brands. We often judge clothes based on whether that tag visibly says DKNY, Adidas, or whichever brand happens to be "in." Maybe people feel a little better and cooler when they walk around with someone else's name brand on their bodies.

In the past, people were their *own* brand. Well-to-do girls were expected to label every item in their hope chest with their maiden name initials. Cross-stitch was most often used, but chain stitch and a range of other stitching types were also popular. Antique bed linens are often decorated exquisitely.

Until the second half of the last century, many homes contained an embroidery reference guide, with patterns and monograms for this tradition.

## cross-stitch

Toward the end of the 19th century, a cross-stitch craze broke out across a range of Western countries. Everything was covered in cross-stitch. Cushions, pillows, carpets, chair seats, suspenders, shoes, slippers, and even boots were awash in cross-stitch, mostly following German or Victorian patterns.

An artist embroidered this bomber jacket to make a political statement about the military.

A traditional design of roses, oak leaves, acorns, and violets decorates these women's stockings from about 1832. The white stocking is machine made, while the design is hand embroidered.

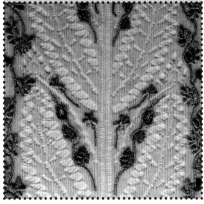

Folklore in high fashion. This embroidered coat with boots was in a Louis Vuitton spring collection.

Why carry around other people's brands when you have a perfectly good one of your own? Here the creator's name is sewn in cross-stitch.

Special embroidery yarn can be used, but you don't need to buy a specific kind. Basically, you can embroider with any thread or yarn you want. Regular sewing thread is fine, and so are wool and cotton yarns. In many cases, the surprise use of a curious material makes it more interesting.

# MATERIALS & STITCHES

To create a unique look, you can embroider with threads from an unraveled woven textile: unraveled silk or organza gives threads that are stronger, yet even finer than sewing thread. String, cord, ribbon, and thin leather bands are also useful for decorating. Attach these thicker yarns to your fabric by sewing over the thick yarn with a thinner thread. This is called *couching*.

## The needle

For bead embroidery, use extra-long, thin needles. The only other ground rule for needles is that they should be somewhat thicker than double the yarn you're using. You want the needle to make the hole in the material, not the yarn.

## The scissors

Embroidery scissors should be small and sharp. Never cut paper with the same pair: they'll become dull and hard to cut yarn with.

## Transferring patterns

There are several ways to transfer patterns onto textiles. You can also experiment with simply drawing directly on your material with a pen, and with free-hand embroidery, using your needle as a "brush."

1. Use dressmaker's carbon and a tracing wheel (available in sewing specialty stores): position pattern right-side up on fabric and pin at each corner. Carefully slip dressmaker's carbon, carbon side down, between fabric and pattern. Draw over the lines of the pattern, using a tracing wheel. You may find that a knitting needle, used like a pencil, will give you more control than the tracing wheel when you are drawing over lines.

2. Use templates, for the most common historical method. People would use things they had on hand, such as saucers, cups, and plates. For example, you can create a floral string by placing half-circles on alternating sides of a straight line to make a winding "stem." Then place smaller circles intermittently along the stem-line to represent the flowers, like a daisy chain or twisting rose vine.

3. Use hot-iron transfer. Copy your design on heavy tracing paper. Turn the paper over. On the back side, trace over your lines with a transfer pencil (available in sewing specialty stores). To see through the paper, tape it, blank side facing you, to a window. With the traced side down on the fabric, press transfer with an iron on low setting for a few seconds. A wax crayon can be used instead of a transfer pencil, but usually produces a thick line, so it is recommended only for large designs on coarse fabrics.

## Nine useful stitches

There are hundreds of different kinds of stitches from all over the world. We've chosen nine of the most common and useful stitch types to begin with. Some can be used both to sew material together, and to create decorative patterns. There are many reference books on embroidery if you would like to learn more than what is outlined here. Refer to page 89 for some recommendations. Even better, you can take a class!

## Running stitch

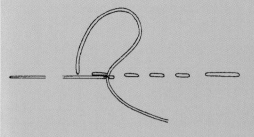

Simply pass your needle up and down through the material. Sew a few rows next to each other for added interest. Try varying the lengths of the stitches for a different effect. The running stitch may be used to attach two pieces of felted fabric. Place the pieces side by side and overlapping 2.5 cm (1 inch). Use a contrasting thread for interest.

**Running stitch in dense rows with silver thread makes a cool ribbed look.**

**Scarf made using a quilting technique. Thin strips have been joined together with running stitch.**

## Backstitch

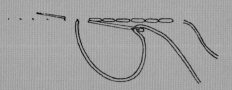

Start by bringing the needle up through the material, on the line you are going to sew. Then push the needle back through, 2.5 cm (1/8 inch) forward along the line, and up again 2.5 cm (1/8 inch) behind the first spot. Make sure the stitches are quite close together, since those on the reverse will be twice as long as those on the top side.

**Appliqué fastened and embroidered with backstitch.**

## Stem stitch

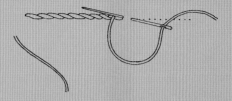

The stem stitch is a backstitch primarily used to outline, letters for example, but is often used to work stems in floral designs as well. Working from left to right, bring the needle out at the starting point. Insert the needle about 1.2 cm (1/2 inch) to the right on the line and bring it out again half a stitch length back. Keep the thread or yarn below the line and below the needle as you work. This process of moving a step back before each new step forward along the line is distinctive in backstitches. Repeat these steps, making sure each stitch length is equal.

**Typical stem stitch embroidery.**

## chain stitch

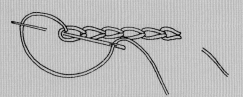

Start by bringing the needle up through the material, on the line you are going to sew. Next, push the needle down right beside where you brought it up, then up again 2.5 cm (1/8 inch) farther along the line. Before you pull the thread through, place the thread under the needle and then pull. Don't pull too hard; let it form a neat loop. Continue the chain by pushing the needle down inside each new loop, and don't forget to place the thread under the needle before you pull.

**Appliqué skull, with the bones sewn in chain stitch.**

## satin stitch

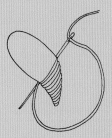

Satin stitch is perfect for filling a small area of embroidery. The stitches are always sewn densely, hiding the base as completely as possible. They can go in any direction, diagonally or in a straight line.

Push the needle up on one side of the outlined shape and down on the other, so the stitches end up being the same length on the reverse as on the top side.

**A monogram in satin stitch.**

## cross-stitch

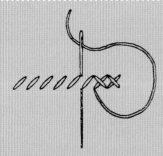

Basic cross-stitch can be formed in two ways. It can be worked in rows of even, slanted stitches, with one arm of the crosses laid down in one run, the other in a second, return run.

Cross-stitches can also be worked one at a time. Work cross-stitches in a row when they are beside each other. Work them singly when they are scattered, to prevent long yarns on the back side of your work. All the top yarns of the cross should lie in the same direction.

**Cross-stitch is great for initials or small pictures.**

## French knots

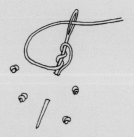

Start by bringing the needle up through the material, where you want a knot. Twist the thread around the needle three times, then push the needle down through the material right next to where you brought it up, and a knot will form.

**A number made of tightly placed French knots, making it look like terrycloth. The number is embroidered on two pieces of material as an appliqué.**

## Blanket stitch

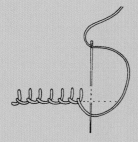

This stitch is worked from left to right on two parallel lines. Bring the needle out on the bottom line and insert on the top line and slightly (about .5 cm or 1/4 inch) to the right, then out directly below on the bottom line. Before pulling the needle through, carry yarn under the point of the needle. Pull until the yarn lies flat on the fabric and proceed to make the next stitch in the same way along the row. Keep the height of the stitches even.

Blanket stitch is useful for attaching appliqué or reinforcing an edge or trim.

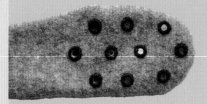

**Mirror ornamentation (mirrors available in sewing specialty shops). Wrap a small plastic or rubber ring (from a hardware store) with blanket stitch. Place the ring on a mirror, then sew the pieces to your material with basting stitches.**

**Decorative edging in blanket stitch.**

## couching stitch

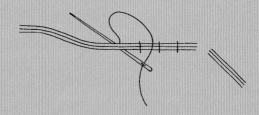

Couching is a method of attaching thicker yarns to the fabric and so giving a single line more weight. Usually, there are two working yarns, the thicker laid yarn (which can be one or more strands) and the thinner couching yarn. The couching yarn is stitched over the laid yarn to attach it to the fabric. The term "couching" comes from the French verb *coucher,* which means to lie down.

Starting from the right, bring the laid yarn up from the back of the fabric with a large-eyed needle. Use left thumb to hold and guide the laid yarn. Bring couching yarn up beside the laid yarn but slightly below it and about .5 cm (1/4 inch) farther left than the starting place of the laid yarn. Make small stitches over the laid yarn about .5 cm apart all the way along, until the laid yarn is completely anchored. Take the laid yarn to the back of the fabric with the large-eyed needle and secure both ends with a few small stitches. Do not clip the laid yarn too close, or it will pop up to the front side of the fabric.

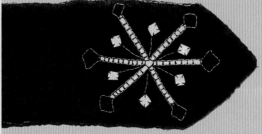

**This mitt is embellished with a reflective material, attached with couching stitches.**

The skirt is decorated with cursive letters made from wool yarn and couching stitch. The hearts are fastened with blanket stitch, and the knitted hat follows the directions on pages 68–69. Dog leashes are fun creations, using pompoms, beads, braids, and tassels.

## Beads and sequins

You can sew beads on one by one, or you can attach a string of beads by sewing couching stitches between the beads.

## Appliqué

A decorative technique where cut-out shapes are sewn onto a base using various stitches. Experiment with any variation of blanket stitch, backstitch, running stitch, or even tiny slip stitches. Slip stitches are small connecting stitches, which are usually invisible. Use them when you want to attach a cut-out shape, but don't want to draw attention to the stitches. To do a slip stitch, catch the edge of the cut-out fabric with small stitches, evenly spaced.

## Machine embroidery

Of course, you can always use the stitches programmed in your sewing machine to embroider. It won't give you quite the same feeling as a hand-stitched item, but it can save a little time.

## Quilting

This is a method of joining several layers of material, often using stuffing, or wadding, in between. The pieces are held together by a variety of stitches that create decorative patterns on the top surface.

Embroidering with tiny beads threaded on a strand is an age-old technique. Remnants of bead embroidery have been found in graves as old as 1500 BCE. The method is still used in folkloric traditions around the world, from African bush peoples to North American First Nations, to Greenland Inuit.

Bead embroidery, like bead knitting and crocheting, became highly fashionable during the 1800s. Accessories such as purses, wallets, belts, slippers, and shoes were all heavily adorned with beads.

**Check out styles from other cultures. Your creativity might be inspired by the colors of a bright Mexican blanket or a beautifully patterned Japanese kimono, the intricate beads and embroidery on an Indian sari, or the subtle textures of a Nepalese scarf. You can also incorporate such materials into your designs.**

**Embroidered boots from the 1860s.**

**1.**

**5.**

**2.**

**6.**

**3.**

**7.**

**9.**

**4.**

**8.**

**10.**

# *Mary Maxim* GRAPH STYLE SWEATER PATTERN

This pattern is complete with graphs for **BOTH** Raglan and Set-in Sleeve styles!

PRICE 25¢

USE ONLY

*Mary Maxim* 4 PLY NORTHLAND WOOL COLOR FAST SHRINE RESISTANT

FOR THIS PATTERN

• COLOR FAST • SHRINK-RESISTANT • LONG-WEARING

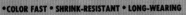

Back View

No. 415 **TOTEM POLE**

MEN'S 4 PLY CARDIGAN
(ZIPPER FRONT)
Sizes: 38 - 40 - 42 - 44

AN ORIGINAL SWEATER DESIGN BY *Mary Maxim*

In the 1940s, '50s, and '60s, a homemade motif sweater (like the one pictured above) was the fashion envy of many. This Mary Maxim sweater design from 1957 could be ordered through the mail.

(top right) Japanese designer Jahji Yamamoto showcased a whole collection of soft knits.

(right) Coco Chanel — a pioneer of comfortable fashion.

# KNITTING

We don't know for certain when and where people began knitting, but the earliest known examples came from Asia around 200 CE.

The technique traveled to continental Europe a few hundred years later, with the adoption of mittens knit in wool or silk. These early mittens would have been used mainly by popes and bishops during religious ceremonies.

European royalty began importing knitted silk stockings in the 14th century. Ordinary people didn't start knitting until the 1700s.

## Namesake island sweaters

Island-dwelling northerners have traditionally fished for a living, but during harsh winter weather when the sea was too dangerous, knitting became a way to bring in extra income.

Various islands developed their own signature patterns and colors. Iceland, Ireland, the Shetland Islands, Jersey, Guernsey, and Arran are examples of some islands that have given their names to special sweater styles.

By wearing their traditional sweaters, fishermen displayed their homelands in foreign ports—a practical way of identification among strangers speaking different languages.

## Knitting takes off

In the 1940s and 1950s, more and more people in the West could afford to spend time enjoying leisure activities and being outdoors.

Knitting in the home quickly became a favorite hobby, with women (and some men) knitting wool sweaters, mittens, toques, and socks. Since knitted clothes are warm and breathable, they're practical and comfortable for many northern winter activities such as skiing, hockey, or skating—or just spending time outside!

## Chanel made fashion comfortable

In the world of fashion, knit materials remained in the shadows until the 1920s, when Coco Chanel (1883–1971), a world-renowned fashion creator, began making pant-suits out of jersey, a soft, machine-made wool tricot.

"Women have to be able to move," was one of Chanel's famous statements, and so she created elegant fashions for ordinary women to live and work in.

# HOW TO KNIT

These basic instructions should give you enough to get started on your knitting project. But there is always more to learn! On page 89, you will find some recommended books on knitting techniques. You may also find it easier to learn in a class, or from someone who knows knitting. To learn how to knit, you need to familiarize yourself with some abbreviations. These are the most common ones:

St = stitch

K = knit

P = purl

KP = knit and purl

You might have a half-finished scarf lying around somewhere that you know is never going to be finished. Or a stretched-out, unattractive knitted item that is actually made with very attractive yarn.

Well, guess what? Now is the perfect time to unravel and reuse that yarn!

If the yarn is too thin for your knitting needles, you can reuse other materials instead—thin strips of material, strong embroidery thread, metal thread, or even kitchen string. Or mix two kinds of yarn together. The key is to not think there is a "correct" way, and to test and experiment to get as close as you can to the picture in your mind's eye.

## changing knitting needle size for effect

The relative looseness—and size—of your garment will depend on how loosely or tightly you knit and on how thick your needles are. If you like the look of a sleeve or skirt that flares at the bottom, you can gradually increase the size of your needles to create the flare.

## checking the tension

If you're knitting from a pattern, you'll need to check the tension—that means the number of stitches and rows you should have in a measured area using the designated yarn and needles.

Knitting instructions will always specify a tension. This is how you ensure that you end up with the right-sized garment. If your tension is different, you can change it by adjusting the size of your needles.

Knit a test piece with the number of stitches and rows given in the tension directions. If you've knitted more tightly, the piece will be too small—switch to thicker needles. If you've knitted more loosely, the piece will be too large—switch to thinner needles.

## Loop cast on

You can cast on using one or two needles. If you cast on with double needles, the first row will be easier to knit.

First, make a slip knot, a simple knot that can be tightened by tugging on one end. At least 15 cm (6 inches) from the end of the yarn, make a loop, leaving a loose end hanging down. The yarn will cross, forming an X. Grab the strand on the top of the X, below the point where the strands cross. Bring it behind and through the first loop. Pull the second loop through the first. This is your slip knot.

Then, with your right hand, grab both needles and slide them through the slip knot. Tighten by tugging the loose end of the yarn. This counts as your first cast-on stitch.

Lift the yarn with your left index finger moving away from you. Catch the strand behind your index finger. Tighten the loop. Repeat until you have as many stitches as you need. Leave a 12 cm (5-inch) tail.

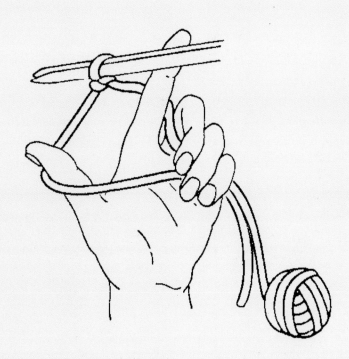

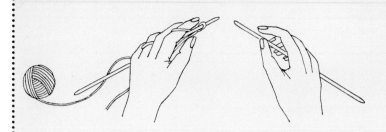

## Hand positioning as you knit

When you've done the cast-on on double needles, pull one of the needles out and hold it in your right hand. The needle with the stitches on it goes in your left hand. Place the yarn over your left index finger, under your middle finger and over your ring finger.

## Knit stitch = K

1. Hold the needle with cast-on stitches in the left hand. Take the yarn behind the work, insert the right needle into the front of the first stitch from left to right so that the right needle now points towards the back. Take the yarn under the right needle, then over the top from left to right. Draw the loop on the right needle forward through the stitch.

2. Allow the first stitch to slide off the left needle. The new stitch remains on the right needle.

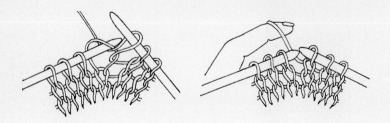

## Purl = P

1. Hold the needle with cast-on stitches in the left hand. Hold the yarn in front of the work. Insert right needle into the front of the first stitch from right to left so that the needle points upward slightly. Take the yarn around the right needle from the forward position and counter clockwise. Draw the loop on the right needle through the stitch, moving it away from you to the back of the work.

2. Allow the first stitch to slide off the left needle. The new stitch remains on the right needle.

## Increase 1

1. Knit into the front and back of the next stitch, as follows: insert the needle into the next stitch as if to knit. Knit this stitch.

2. Do not slide the stitch off the needle, but instead, insert the right needle into the back of the same stitch. Knit this stitch. Now slide the stitch off the needle. This makes one increase.

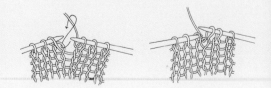

## Increase 2

This method is best when you want to increase by several stitches at the end of a row or to make button or thumb holes. You just create new stitches by wrapping loops on the needle. Then, while knitting the next row, simply knit onto these "loop stitches" as you would onto regular stitches.

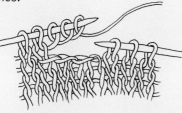

## Decrease

1. Knit 2 stitches together as you would a single stitch.
2. Your decrease will lean to the right.

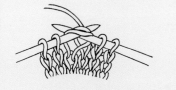 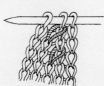

## Decrease by crossing stitches

1. Lift a stitch from the left to the right needle (as if you were going to do a knit stitch), but without pulling any yarn through.
2. Knit the next stitch as you normally would.
3. Pull the lifted stitch over the knit stitch.
4. Your decrease will lean to the left.

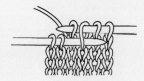 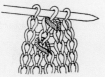

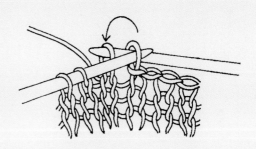

## casting off

1. Knit 2 knit stitches at the beginning of a row.
2. Pull the first knit stitch over the other one and off the needle.
3. One stitch will remain on the needle. Knit a new stitch so you have 2 stitches again; pull one over the other as before.
4. Repeat until you have one remaining stitch, making the cast-off row slightly looser than the rest of the knitting. Cut off the yarn, pull the end through the last stitch, and tie a knot.

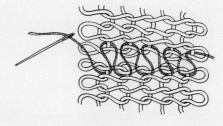

## Assembling knits

When you want to sew two pieces of knitting together, you stitch them on the right side. Sew one row in from the edge, onto the crossways line between the stitches, then onto exactly the same spot on the opposite side.

Push the needle down again right next to where you brought it up in the last stitch. Sew a few stitches at a time, then pull a bit to tighten, and the stitches will disappear into the knit.

# KNITTING & RECYCLING

Fuzzy against smooth. This skirt is decked out in a knitted-on mohair flounce, attached by pulling up stitches tightly along the edge. The embroidery is in the same mohair yarn, with chain stitch and glass beads.

This sweater was too tight around the neck. The neckline was scooped out, stitches picked up along its edge, and a new striped, ribbed collar attached. The center decoration used appliqué technique with pieces of a white sweater.

## New parts knitted onto an old sweater

Sometimes you might want to just extend or change the cuffs, hem, or neckline on an existing sweater.

Unravel the stitches at the edge with a crochet hook and transfer them onto a knitting needle. Gently release one stitch at a time by un-picking them with a needle or crochet hook. Now you can add any trim you like. Turn the trim into a ruffle if you want, by pulling your stitches tightly up toward the edge; the knit will become wavy as you start knitting.

You can give a garment a whole new look by contrasting fuzzy with smooth, thin with thick, or striped with a single color. Or you can change its function by playing with length: a sweater can be extended to make a dress; an old lamb's wool pullover can be updated with a wide turtleneck.

## cuffs of all shapes and sizes

Cuffs are among the easiest things to knit. You can knit them loosely and combine them in different ways for different uses. If you make a very large, loose cuff, it could be used as a type of poncho to cover your shoulders, as a tube dress, or as a "hip warmer" if you pull it down farther. It all depends on you ...

Experiment combining your custom "cuffs" with accessories, such as scarves, necklaces, or belts. And, of course, if you knit standard-sized cuffs as wrist and leg warmers, they'll add color and texture contrast to your outfits.

## How to knit cuffs

Rib stitches are produced by alternating knit and purl in one row. To make wide rib stitches on your cuffs, use a 2X2 rib stitch, that is, K2, P2, using 3.5 needles. When the piece is as long as you'd like it, simply sew it together to form a cuff.

If you use 180 stitches, the cuff can be used as a yoke-style poncho, a strapless tank, or a miniskirt, depending on your size. If it turns out tighter than you want it, try using the same directions with thicker needles. To get a specific size, knit a test piece to check the tension, and take your body measurements to estimate how many stitches you need to cast on.

## Knitted cords

A knitted cord is both strong and elastic and has many, many uses— as shoelaces, handles for purses, drawstrings for pants or bags ... In the past, people even knit their own clotheslines.

## How to knit a cord

To knit a cord you'll need double-point needles, which are also used for socks or mittens. Cast on 3–6 stitches, depending on how thick the yarn and the needles are, and how thick you want the cord to be.

Using only knit stitches, finish the first row. At the end of row 1, don't switch the work as you would with regular needles; instead, push the stitches to the other end of the needle. This way, you always have the right side of the piece toward you.

Knit the stitches from the same direction once again. Continue in the same way with each row. By pulling the yarn tight on the backside of the work, the knit will start to curl into a round cord after a few rows.

The wrist warmer above was knit using #3 needles and ribbing technique.

Sack made from a patterned sweater. The pattern has been highlighted with bead embroidery. A knitted cord serves as handle.

## Bead knitting

Bead knitting is one of the most fun ways to revive a garment. And bead knit pieces can be combined with reused sweaters in many different ways. You can also experiment with adding other bits and pieces — nuts of different sizes, thin plastic rings sawed from old coloring pens or straws — instead of beads. Or thread on little pieces of felt, buttons.... or whatever you have lying around at home.

## How to knit with beads

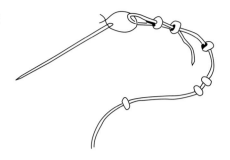

Using only knit stitches, start by threading the beads onto the yarn you're knitting with. To make it easier to thread the beads on, you can use a needle. If the beads are tight, you might have to use sewing thread to get the needle on, which you then link to the yarn.

Start by knitting a row without beads. In the next row, when you have the backside toward you, you start knitting in the beads. First, knit a regular stitch, then feed on one of the beads from the yarn and push it down toward the right needle and the right side of the piece. Knit

another stitch, and repeat. The beads will sit between the stitches.

Carry on this pattern of knitting one row without beads, and adding beads in every other row. Or you can choose to add the beads in another pattern, if you like. Knitting quite tightly produces the best bead knit effect.

**Wrist warmer with knit "antennae." You can crochet up from stitches anywhere on a knit bottom to create "sprouts" like these, using the same method as for a knitted cord.**

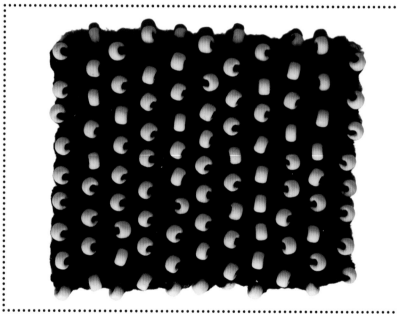

**Black wrist warmer with yellow beads knitted in.**

## Strip knitting

Just like you can make rugs out of cotton cut into rags, you can knit using cut-up recycled sweaters. Cut long strips, which you can cut again into shorter bits, depending on how long you want the "fringe" to be.

You use exactly the same method as for bead knitting, but instead of feeding on a bead, pass a strip under the knitting yarn just before making a stitch. Hold both ends up while making the stitch before continuing with the next stitch.

Remember to always use only knit stitches. The more tightly you knit, the better the strips will stay in place and the more sturdy the fringe will turn out to be.

## Shag knitting

Instead of using strips of recycled sweater, you can tie bits of used yarn onto your main yarn. Keep feeding the knots through one at a time, just like with the beads and strips, and you'll get a shaggy look. Experiment with the length of yarn bits, and how many you use, to try different effects.

*Note: Each of these methods can by used to embellish any pattern you are following, as long as it calls for knit stitches only.*

## Knitted Hat with or without earflaps

**Needles:** 2 regular number 6 needles

**Knitting technique:** knit stitches only

**Tension:** 16.5 sts and 29 rows = 10x10 cm (4x4 inches)

**Yarn:** medium thick

**Size:** one size fits all. The hat will be about 20 cm (8 inches) from top to bottom, and very stretchy. For a tighter hat, use thinner needles; for a longer hat, cast on additional stitches.

## Instructions

Cast on 34 stitches.

Row 1: Knit the entire row except the last stitch, which you leave on the left needle. Turn.

Row 2: Lift the first stitch over without knitting it. Knit the rest of the stitches until the end of the row. Turn.

Row 3: Knit the whole row except the last 2 stitches. Turn.

Row 4: Lift the first stitch over without knitting it. Knit the rest of the stitches until the end of the row. Turn.

Row 5: Knit the whole row except the last 3 stitches. Turn.

Rows 6–13: Continue in the same way: On even rows, lift the first stitch over without knitting it, then knit the whole row. Turn. On odd rows, knit almost the whole row but decrease each time, saving an increasing number of stitches on the left needle, until you've accumulated 7 leftover stitches.

Row 14: Lift the first stitch over without knitting it. Knit the rest of the stitches until the end of the row. Turn.

Row 15: Knit up to the leftover stitches; this time, you'll knit these, too, proceeding as follows: Knit 1 stitch, then pick up an extra stitch in the middle, before the next stitch. Set it on the left needle, and stitch it along with the next stitch. Repeat this picking up of in-between stitches until all the leftover stitches are done. (Note: You can skip this step if you're a beginner and simply knit the left-over stitches as usual; however, when the hat is done, you'll want to sew up the gaps that remain using needle and thread.)

Row 16: Lift the first stitch over without knitting it. Knit the rest of the stitches until the end of the row. Turn.

If you're adding earflaps, start the first one at this stage.

If you're not, complete the hat by simply repeating rows 1–16 seven more times. Cast off, and sew up the hat at the back.

## Instructions for earflaps

When Row 16 is done, add 4 new "loop stitches" using the Increase 2 technique (see p. 63). Turn.

Row 17: Knit across these 4 new stitches and complete the row according to the main instructions for Row 1. Turn.

Row 18: Knit the entire row, then add an additional 4 loop stitches.

Row 19: Knit across these 4 new stitches and complete the row according to the main instructions for Row 3. Turn.

Rows 20–30: Knit according to the main instructions for Rows 4–14. Turn.

Row 31: Cast off 4 stitches. Knit the new stitches, then complete the row according to the main instructions for Row 15. Turn.

Row 32: Knit the entire row. Turn.

Row 33: Cast off 4 stitches. Knit the new stitches, then complete the row according to the main instructions for Row 1. Turn.

Rows 34–48: Knit according to the main instructions for Rows 2–16.

Complete the earflap by repeating Rows 1 through 16 in the main instructions three times more, and then a last repetition of Rows 2–16 in the main instructions. The second earflap is completed using exactly the same steps. Cast off, and sew up the hat at the back.

Personalize your hat with blanket stitch or crochet trim, or add ties, braids, or tassels.

Rag-knit hat. Wooly strips in two tones were knitted onto the wool hat base.

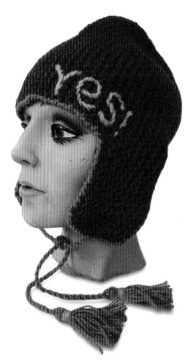

The same base hat but without "fur"; this one is embroidered using stem stitch. The edges are crocheted, and the ties are made of two coiled knit cords with tassels.

(top left) An antique purse, crocheted in wool yarn and silk.

(above) Frequent traveling, from Aspen to Vail, Jasper and Whistler, turned these two big-mountain free-skiers into crochet maniacs. Sverre Liliequsit and Kaj Zackrisson founded their own brand, Kask, in 2001 and sell their hats, headbands, and visors all over the world.

This fashion design student, modeling her own clothes, combines knitting and crocheting in the same garment.

# CROCHETING

Crocheted dresses from the 1960s.

Crochet's journey through history has been anything but trouble-free. Crochet was only popularized in the late 19th century, when cotton yarn became affordable for the first time. Crochet enthusiasts quickly produced everything from skullcaps to bedspreads and tablecloths.

People who consider themselves defenders of good taste have sometimes seen crochet as an unappealing handicraft, while others have passionately kept up the practice.

In the '60s and '70s, crochet became a huge trend. If you were in the know, you would have crocheted everything from dresses, shawls, and hats to color-intense squares sewn together to make vests and sweaters.

Today we see a similar trend, with contemporary twists. Even guys are grabbing crochet hooks and getting started, with extreme sport athletes leading the way.

Skirt made of sewn-together strips of cut-up sweater sleeves, and decorated with crochet circles.

# HOW TO CROCHET

Like knitting, crochet instructions usually use abbreviations. Here are the most common ones:

| | |
|---|---|
| ST | stitch |
| CH | chain stitch |
| SC | single crochet |
| DC | double crochet |

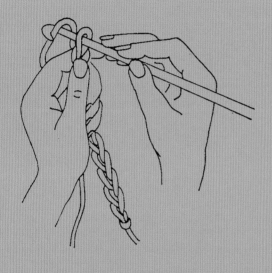

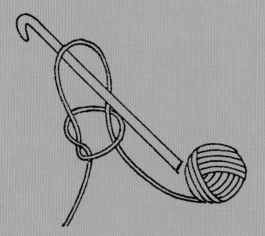

The following instructions are enough to show you basic crocheting, but see page 89 for a list of further reading. Before you can start, you need to make a special slipknot, as shown. Push the hook through the knot and pull on the long yarn end to adjust the size.

## chain stitch

Creating a row of chain stitches is always the starting point for any crochet project.

Hold the crochet hook in your right hand just like you would hold a pen and hold the slipknot and the yarn in your left.

1. Push the hook under the yarn from the front, catch the yarn (also called "yarn over"), and twist the hook downward, so it will go through more easily.
2. Pull the hook with the yarn back through the loop. You've now completed one chain stitch.

## Single crochet

When you've made as many chain stitches as you need, make one extra chain stitch, and turn the piece around. This extra chain stitch ensures that the edge of the crochet piece turns out straight.

1. Push the hook through the 3rd chain stitch (count the first chain stitch as the one sitting on the hook) and yarn over.

2. Draw the hook with the yarn back through the chain; now you will have 2 loops on the hook. Push the hook through again and yarn over. Pull the hook with the yarn back through both chain stitches. You've now completed a single crochet stitch.

3. Push the hook into the next chain stitch and repeat steps 1–3 for all the chain stitches in the row.

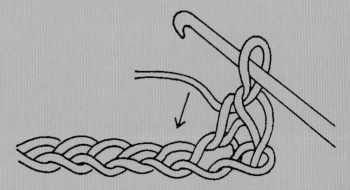

You've made a row of single crochet stitches. Before you turn the piece and start the next row, remember to make an extra chain stitch for the edge to remain flush.

## Double crochet

When you've made as many chain stitches as you need, make 2 extra chain stitches and turn the piece around. The extra chain stitches ensure that the edge of the piece turns out straight—because double crochet stitches are taller than single ones, you must make 2 extra chain stitches.

1. Yarn over.

2. Push the hook through the 5th chain stitch (count the first chain stitch as the one sitting on the hook), yarn over again, and pull the hook with the yarn back through the chain. Now you will have 3 loops on the hook.

3. Yarn over, and pull the hook with the yarn back through the last 2 loops on the hook.

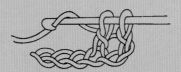

4. Yarn over a last time, and pull the hook with the yarn back through the last 2 chain stitches. You've now completed a double crochet stitch. Crochet one double stitch in each of the chain stitches. Remember to add 2 chain stitches before you turn the work to do the next row.

## Creating different textures in crochet

To create texture on a crocheted surface, you can crochet into the back of the chain, or into the front of the chain—or into both front and back to create different looks. Experiment to create various textures.

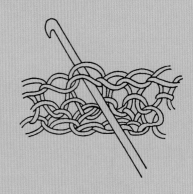

## Scalloped edging

Start with 1 single crochet stitch on the edge of your piece, skip 1 stitch, and then make 1 on the next stitch. Crochet 4 additional single stitches onto this same stitch, skip 1 stitch, crochet 1 single stitch, and so on.

**Skirt made from a fisherman's sweater, with scalloped crochet edging and belt loops added.**

**Arm warmers with buttons and scalloped crochet edging.**

## corded edging

This type of edging crochet is very firm and neat; in the past, it was used to strengthen the edges of washing rags. It's called corded crochet because working in the opposite direction you normally would creates an edge that looks like a cord.

Push the hook through near the edge of your item, and yarn over to the right side, creating 1 stitch on the hook. Continue by pushing the hook through again a bit to the right of the last stitch and yarn over again, pulling the yarn through to the right side. Now you have 2 stitches on your hook. Yarn over again and pull the yarn through both loops. Repeat, always working left to right.

**Crocheted trim and ornamental circles.**

## Diamond mesh

Mesh squares are formed from chain stitches secured with either single or double crochet stitches.

If you want to add a mesh piece to an existing sweater sleeve, the result will be sturdier if you begin by adding a row of chain stitches around the edge and use that as a base. If it is hard to push your hook through the material, start with an embroidered blanket stitch edging instead, then crochet onto that.

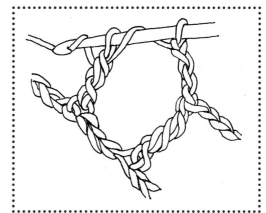

**Network crocheting, where each chain stitch sequence is attached with double knots.**

**Network-crocheted wrist warmer made from chain stitch half-circles. Every new half-circle is fastened with a secure stitch in the middle of the previous half circle.**

## crocheted flowers and other shapes

Crochet is well suited to freestanding shapes. You can crochet a flower or a series of circles, even figures, long cords, necklaces, or bracelets. The sky is the limit with crochet!

Combine crochet shapes with beads, buttons, tassels, or flowing tufts or yarn. Sew them right onto the garment you're working on, or attach them with safety pins so you can move them around.

## crochet clusters and flowers

Crochet several chain stitches and join them to form a ring. Crochet around and around the center with single or double crochet stitches, as it will change the look of the cluster. Create floral shapes by using single and double crochet interchangeably. Remember that at the end of every row, you will need to increase a few stitches to make the circles larger and larger. This way the clusters will remain flat.

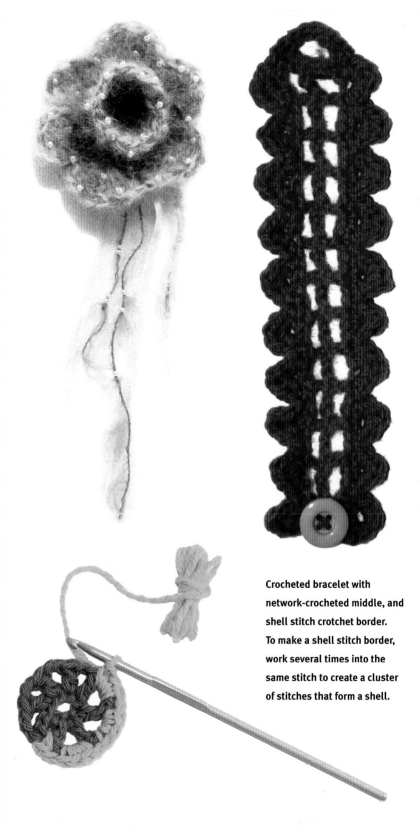

**Crocheted bracelet with network-crocheted middle, and shell stitch crotchet border. To make a shell stitch border, work several times into the same stitch to create a cluster of stitches that form a shell.**

# DETAILING

A piece of clothing can be fine on its own, but often, small detailing will make a garment truly unique. An asymmetrical finish on a sleeve, a bold fringe, or a special button can be the icing on the cake.

**H**ere are a few tips and ideas to start you off. You can add your custom signature to your clothes in an endless variety of ways ...

## Roses

Cut an oblong piece of material and roll it loosely while you gather the bottom between your fingers. Sew it together at the bottom with a few stitches. Open up the rose by separating the "petals," using your fingers or a pair of scissors.

Make solo flowers for a single decorative "brooch" or an entire bouquet, maybe even adding some leaf shapes. Sew or glue them onto a safety pin or brooch pin base so you can use them with different outfits.

## Yarn buttons

You can give buttons the look you want by using different yarn textures and qualities— shiny or fuzzy, thin or thick. You can also decorate them with beads and sequins and make them into real gems.

Plastic and metal hoops are available in different sizes in most hobby and sewing specialty shops. Sew a dense blanket stitch around the ring itself, twisting any loose ends inward as you go. Wrap another color yarn across the ring so the pieces cross in the middle like spokes in a wheel. Next, sew around each of the diagonals in the middle until the ring is filled.

The button will look different on both sides: choose the one you like best for the front.

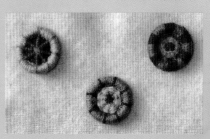

Pompom coat by Alexander McQueen, British fashion guru.

## Pompoms

Cut out 2 round cardboard pieces; they should be 2.5 cm (1 inch) or so larger than you want the pompom to be. Make a hole in the middle of both pieces and lay them against each other. Wrap thick (double or triple) yarn through the center, using a needle or your fingers, until the hole is filled.

Cut the yarn between the cardboard pieces, following around the circle. Wrap a few rounds of strong sewing thread between the pieces, pull them tight, and tie a secure knot.

Cut the cardboard pieces out of the yarn and discard. Steam and fluff the pompom, and it will come out evenly round.

## Make a bunch of pompoms at once

To make several pompoms at once, turn a chair upside down and wind yarn around the legs to desired thickness. Keep the yarn tight while winding. More yarn makes a thicker pompom.

Tie a tight knot around the bunch every 5–8 cm (2–3 inches), using strong thread. Cut the yarn halfway between each knot. Fluff and steam each pompom separately.

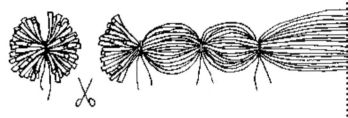

The final step of steaming is important to fill and even out your pompoms. Hold the pompoms carefully over boiling water, and roll them like cookie dough in the palm of your hand. Finish evening them out at the end with scissors, if you need to.

## Tasseled fringe

Make several small bundles of yarn, all the same length. Fold them double and pull them through the edge where you want them, so a loop is formed. Pull one end of the yarn bundle through, then tie a knot that is snug up to the edge, making sure each side is the same length.

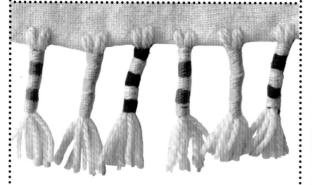

## Wrapped tassels

Attach tasseled fringes as described above. Then cut different thread or yarn colors, all the same length. Wind the thread or yarn around the tassels, starting near the top edge. Finish the tassel by burying the ends inside the tassel with a needle.

Yarn tassels decorate this recycled sweater.

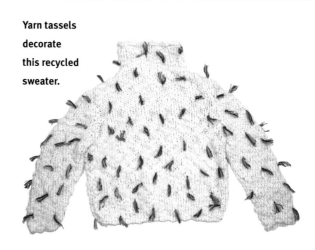

## Knotted tassels

You can knot the tassels in long rows, or in any pattern you choose. It helps to use a ruler or a pen to tie around, to make your pattern completely even. You can also add beads between the knots for extra decoration.

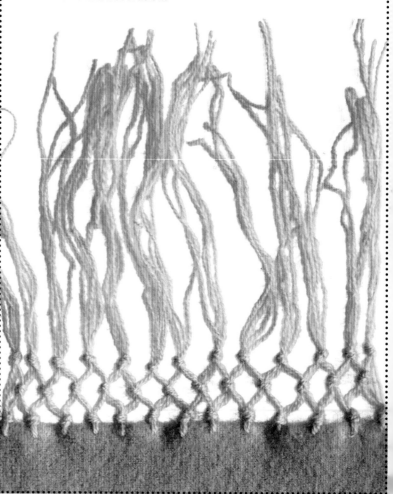

**Standard wool fringe.
You can also leave the
loops uncut.**

## Basic fringe

You need two people to work on this fringe successfully. You need a thick yarn for the fringe and a thinner, strong yarn to secure the fringe. You'll also need a ruler or some other flat rectangular object that will determine the width of your fringe.

Make 2 long loops with the securing yarn. Tie the ends of the securing yarn and the ends of the fringing yarn all together into one knot.

Person 1 holds the ruler and the fringe yarn. Person 2 sits opposite, holding one securing yarn loop in each hand.

1. Person 1 holds the knot against the ruler's edge and wraps the fringe yarn once around the ruler.
2. Next, Person 2 threads the left hand's loop through the right-hand one and gives a good tug.

When the whole fringe is done in this manner, tie all the ends securely and cut the fringe at the bottom of the rectangle.

Steam and even out with scissors as needed. (See pompoms for steaming directions.)

To make an extra-thick fringe, you can sew several fringes together. It's easiest to sew them together before you pull the rulers out.

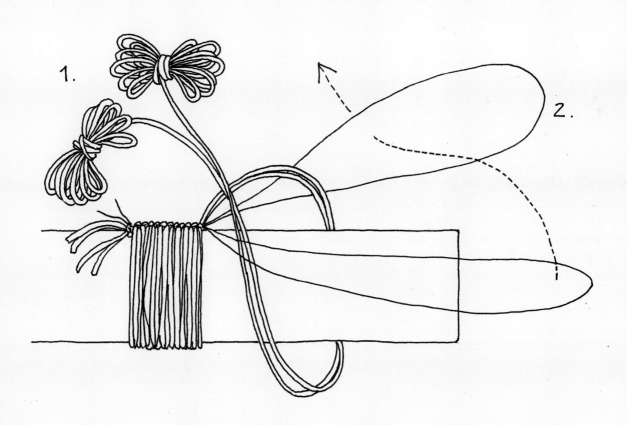

## Twine cord

You'll need a piece of doubled yarn 6 times as long as the cord you want to make.

1. Fasten the doubled yarn to a hook or door handle. Tie the ends together and stick a pen between the pieces.
2. Twist the pen around, twisting in the same direction until the yarn is so tight that it begins to form kinks. Remove the pen and fold the yarn in two, while keeping it tight. Lift the yarn off the hook, hold both ends tight, and release the cord, allowing it to unwind, smoothing out kinks to make it even. The yarn will roll into a cord. Knot both loose ends immediately.

## Oversized tassel

1. Wrap the yarn loosely around a book or piece of cardboard.
2. Thread a strand (or more) of yarn through the top and tie firmly with a knot, leaving one long end for winding and sewing later. Cut the strands at the bottom. Hide the knot, and the short end left over from tying it, under the folded strands.
3. Wind the long strand a few times to secure the folded end, then thread it through so that it comes out the top. Trim ends.

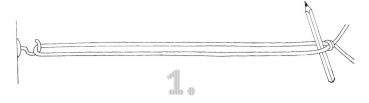

**1.**

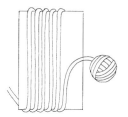

**2.**

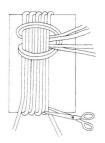

**1.**

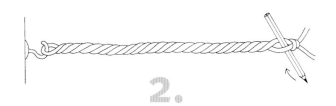

**2.**

**3.**

## Hand-sewn looped edging

This looped edging can be used for both decorative effect and to make buttonholes. The edging needs to be sewn onto a solid rim.

Thread 4 strands of fine but firm yarn, such as cotton, through a needle and secure to the left top edge. Draw out a loop to the desired length and secure in place with a small stitch, from the top side to the bottom side of the edge. Bring the needle through to the top side and continue making these loops all along the edge. Return by making tight blanket stitches around the loops, completely covering the strands. You are now back where you started. Secure the ends. If you're going to use them as button-holes, remember to measure the loops for size before you wrap them in blanket stitch.

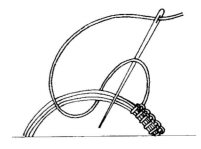

## Holes

With felted sweaters, you have a material that won't unravel when you cut into it, so it can be fun to work with holes, tears, and rips. Just make sure before you start that the material you're cutting is properly felted!

You can even make your own lace patterns. If you cut out larger shapes, you can reinforce the material by appliquéing patches behind the holes. Or sew your lace onto a thin, transparent material. Blanket, basting, and running stitch are all good when working with holes. You can get totally creative ...

Sweater cuff with wrist warmer—its small holes are filled with embroidery, using the yarn button method. The edge is decorated with French knots and running stitch.

Sweater with "lacy" effect. Notches were cut all over the sweater with a pair of small, sharp scissors. When you put it on and pull your arms up, the notches open up.

**Pants from the Middle Ages with peek-a-boo slits**
Court fashion in the 1500s was distinguished by knee-length pants with vented features and a padded crotch. These Spanish pants, knitted by infamous courtier August Von Sachsens, have leather lining and yellow taffeta that wells out of the slits.

With a little imagination and time, you can create one-of-a-kind clothes and have loads of fun. Anyone can do it! You and your friends can even start your own Second-Time Cool custom clothing group.

# Recommended Reading

If you'd like to learn more about any of the techniques outlined in this book, there are many books devoted to knitting, crocheting, and embroidery. The following are good beginner books:

**On knitting**
*Cool Stuff: Teach Me to Knit*
Leisure Arts (Little Rock, AR)

*Knitting*, by Judy Ann Sadler
Kids Can Press (Toronto, ON), 2002

*Stitch 'n Bitch*, by Debbie Stoller
Workman Publishing (New York, NY), 2004

**On crocheting**
*Cool Stuff: Teach Me to Crochet*
Leisure Arts (Little Rock, AR)

*My Crochet Teacher*, by Susan Bates
Coats & Clark (Greer, SC), 1987

*Crocheting*, by Gwen Blakley Kinsler and Jackie Young
Kids Can Press (Toronto, ON), 2003

**On embroidery**
*Embroidery*, by Judy Ann Sadler
Kids Can Press (Toronto, ON), 2004

**General Interest**
*The Jumbo Book of Needlecrafts*
Kids Can Press (Toronto, ON), 2005
This book compiles *Knitting*, *Crocheting* and *Embroidery* with information on quilting and sewing by machine.

Some people find it easier to learn these skills in a class or with a group. Ask at your local yarn or crafts store about knitting, crocheting, or sewing classes offered in your area.

# Index

# Photo credits

cover Waldemar Hansson; facing p. 1 Guy; p. 2 Waldemar Hansson; p. 4 (left) Patrik Johansson, (right) The Nordic Museum; p. 5 (left) The Nordic Museum, (right) Åsa Arvidsson; p. 6 Antoni Ruiz Aragó; p. 7 courtesy of TRAID (Textile Recycling for Aid and International Development) www.traid. org.uk; p. 8 Ulla-Karin Hellsten, The Wool Spinnery of Östergötland; p. 10 Marks & Kattens AB and The Nordic Museum; p. 11 Antoni Ruiz Aragó; p. 12 Waldemar Hansson; pp. 13, 15 Guy; p. 16 Waldemar Hansson; pp. 17–19 Guy; p. 20 Waldemar Hansson; pp. 21–22 Guy; p. 23 (right) Lovikkavanten AB; pp. 24–25 Waldemar Hansson; p. 25 The Nordic Museum; pp. 27–28 Guy; p. 29 Antoni Ruiz Aragó; p. 30 Waldemar Hansson; p. 31 Guy; p. 32 (top) Guy, (bottom) The Nordic Museum; p. 34 Waldemar Hansson; p. 35 (top) Verelst, John/Library and Archives Canada/C-092414, (bottom) Jan Berg, The Textile Museum of Borås, "Grannlåtsväskor" Exhibition, 2003; pp. 36–37 Guy; pp. 38–39 Waldemar Hansson; pp. 40–43 Guy; p. 44 Antoni Ruiz Aragó; p. 45 Elsa Shiaparelli, Musée de la Mode et du Textile / Collection Ufac; p. 46 The Nordic Museum; p. 47 (top left) Peter Johansson / Bus 2004, part of the "Guten Heute alle Leute. Es ist Unser in der Luft. Bald kommen die Löwen und die Bären," artist Peter Johansson, embroidery Ritha Bjarnehall, costume Barbro Scott, Kurbits painting Anne Hjerp, photography Tord Lund, (top middle) The Nordic Museum, (top right) Antoni Ruiz Aragó, (bottom) Guy; pp. 48, 50–54 Guy; p. 55 Waldemar Hansson; p. 56 (left) iStock. com, (right) The Nordic Museum; p. 57 Guy; p. 58 (left) courtesy of Mary Maxim Canada, (top right) Antoni Ruiz Aragó, (bottom right) Pressens Photo; pp. 64–67, 69 Guy; p. 70 (top left) The Nordic Museum, (bottom left) Anna-Stina Lindén Ivarsson, (right) Jan Thorbjörnsson, Rookies; p. 71 Marks & Kattens AB; p. 72 Waldemar Hansson; pp. 76–79 Guy; p. 80 Antoni Ruiz Aragó; pp. 81–86 Guy; p. 87 (top) Guy, (bottom) Livrustkammaren, photographer Göran Schmidt; p. 88 Guy

# About the Authors

**Anna-Stina Lindén Ivarsson** works as a fashion reporter for several major Swedish newspapers and magazines, and has a degree in art criticism.

**Katarina Brieditis** is an industrial and fashion designer, whose practice is driven by the "pleasure of the eye."

**Katarina Evans** is a handicraft specialist with an embroidery focus, who works in the textile industry.

**Maria Lundin** has translated a number of children's books from Swedish, including the young adult novel *God and I Broke Up* (Groundwood, 2005). Maria grew up in Stockholm and now lives in Toronto.

# About the Book

*Second-Time Cool* was developed as part of the Do Redo project by Anna-Stina Lindén Ivarsson, Katarina Breiditis and Katarina Evans. The creators want to show how easy and fun it can be to make something with your own hands through sewing, knitting, embroidery and crocheting. They believe working with these crafts is good for the soul, stimulates the imagination, provides satisfaction and happiness, and makes the world a better place by encouraging everyone to recycle in a creative way. To learn more, go to the website at **www.doredo.se**